Who Sleeps at Night?

Sandra Renew

Who Sleeps at Night?
Poetry of conflict

Who Sleeps at Night?: Poetry of conflict
ISBN 978 1 76041 314 9
Copyright © text Sandra Renew 2017

First published 2017 by
Ginninderra Press
PO Box 3461 Port Adelaide 5015 Australia
www.ginninderrapress.com.au

Contents

Foreword	7
He was shot in his driveway	9
Was there malice?	10
We wore the pink triangle	11
Watching the storm	13
Key turning	14
Crows call Aka Aka	15
Silent combat	16
Across the street	17
After school	18
Regime change	19
Family history	20
Come away sunshine	21
Goths	22
The mirror	23
Iced	24
Ice	25
Lengthen the hem	26
How can a few unresolved chin hairs	27
Doll found in trunk	28
I quail before your peacock gaze	29
Dark net	30
Touch question	31
Mainline west	32
Dangerous to our country	33
At Maralinga	34
Boots on the ground	35
In the Hindu Kush	36
Children dance	37
Can democracy	38

The soldiers and the tea boy	39
Migration	41
Stations of the northern road (1)	42
Stations of the northern road (2)	44
From the sixties real Australians say welcome to refugees	46
Just part of the tragedy	47
Laughing	48
Transition	49
Two degrees	50
El Niño	51
Crops	52
Eyes closed	53
About the Author	54

Foreword

Dissent can be a good thing, unless you are killed for it. In a world of social fissuring and disruption, families and nations are stressed by the contexts we live in. Globally, we are witnessing the biggest population movement ever known. This is interlinked with the causes and effects of massive changes in climate which is causing unresolvable tensions around water and land access, citizenship and poverty.

Armed conflict, fear, persecution and exclusion allow the fermenting of corruption and war.

I write poetry to express contemporary issues and questions of our times about war, language, environment, climate and the planet's health, translation, dislocation, migration, terrorism, border crossings, dissent, gender, protest.

Poetry is a specific way of knowing, of crystallising the dissonance in the dominant discourses in a way which is accessible to anyone who is driven by revolution, and which gives expression to social conscience.

He was shot in his driveway

He was shot in his driveway
in front of his dog.
It was in the season when brumbies
move down the mountains
to protected valleys.
The gun-shy dog was not seen again for months –
not until well after the funeral
held under the river gums at the end of the paddock
where several dry-eyed women dressed in black held hankies
to their eyes –
not until the magpies
carolled in the morning frost and,
missing the autumn rain,
the country was parched.

We wondered, throughout that winter,
who had done it, and why now, and was it a portent
of something for which we should prepare
or a random act of ill will toward him,
a man in an old Akubra, and his dog.

It was not until the arrival
of the season of fires
when fresh green shoots are released
that the child in the old Akubra
stopped asking why…

Was there malice?

Was there malice?
I cannot think there was, although
depending on how you heard it,
you could believe
that four horsemen trampled the flowers,
put paid to the gnome and left the gate wide open.

Was there thoughtlessness?
I cannot say there was, whereas
my sisters tell and retell the story,
one with a small ridged line of muscle down the side of her mouth –
the other, her cowboy trousers torn and grass stained,
vows retribution befitting cataclysm and apocalypse.

Was there an end-of-the-line, stepped-over-the-boundaries feeling?
I cannot say there was, however,
as he stood, taller than the rest of us,
his hair standing up in clumps stiffened with mud,
the expression in my brother's eyes gave us all permission to leave that day.

Depending on who tells it,
despite the loss of face, and because
we all have skin in the game,
it was the beginning, that day, of a new awareness
between the four of us.

We wore the pink triangle

I am running
silent sandshoes on concrete
slipping over the door sill
while he looks for something at random
to lay his hand on

Pine Gap gate
at night the women's protest camp
spotlighted   highlights
peacemakers   while governments
collude in war on war on war

woman in black
nicotine patch matches
biceps tattoos
under the dripping awning
smoking in the rain

in tropic heat
hire car upholstery
exhales chemicals
Every day, visiting your father in the nursing home,
I had to resist driving off this cliff into the sea, she said.

who owns
interpretations
of Auschwitz?
you say 'I'm Jewish'
but we wore the pink triangle

don't we all have
responsibility
to challenge
hatred and violence –
especially in politics?

The Nazi Party in Germany before and during World War II imposed a system of identification badges on internees in their concentration camps. To show outcast status, the Jews wore a yellow star; homosexuals an inverted pink triangle; Gypsies/Roma a brown triangle; a general classification of anti-social (A social), a black triangle. This last group included prostitutes, vagrants, murderers and thieves and those violating laws prohibiting sexual intercourse between Aryans and Jews. Some think lesbians were included in this last group although there is no record of lesbians made to wear the black triangle because of their sexuality. However, some lesbians may have worn the black triangle because they had transgressed in other ways. The marking for sexuality was the pink triangle. Since the 1970s the pink triangle has been taken up as a symbol for gay pride and gay rights. More recently, some LGBTI groups have adopted the black triangle symbol.

Watching the storm

she sees her, a stranger,
sitting on the sand at Bondi
in her burka,
the outline of her knotted up hair
under the black fabric covering

together they contemplate
the wider horizon, distant, unreachable
separated from their beach
by the distant storm,
water, black on black.

key turning

the lid opens outwards
inside hidden
by the dazzle of light –
night still longer than the day

crows call Aka Aka

eldest sister come to our aid
family demands
more and more butterflies cloud high
in the coconut trees

Silent combat

As if having treats was usual, travelling
between Ballarat and Geelong on the Midland Highway,
we littered the back seat vinyl of the Holden –
Mintie wrappers, and Jaffas crushed
into the carpet behind the front seat barrier.
They were busy
in silent combat. Flying under the radar,
we gorged ourselves on sugar
careless of our self-control and fragile teeth.

Across the street

The girl with the crimson hair
the bloke in the bushie's hat
two little girls with dolls and sunhats
and a bitzer dog called Izzie
moved in across the street
trailer loaded: paint chipped iron-frame beds
bundled blankets, cartons of stuff for the kitchen –
locked the gate on the farm, drove two days to get here
a nineteen seventies government cottage
in an unremarkable inner city suburb…
if only we could get a go on he said
she slammed the car door we'll just have to give it a go

after school

after the classroom humiliation
she wrote in fertiliser
on the teacher's lawn
using carefully correct spelling
and waited until the new grass growth
showed FUCK YOU
in bright, bright green

regime change

when the scrappers are pulled apart
and held up by the neck scruffs,
when deep breaths are taken to steady the gasping,
usually, afterwards,
insincere apologies
can be forced from red and teary faces
mumbled in the general direction of the other
and indistinct promises made for future improved behaviour –
at the same time, it is clear
it is not over –
and each will walk away, shoulders tensed
eyes squinted, half closed, shoes kicking up
another threat   watch your back Sunshine
I'm still here

Family history

I know there is little or no use in
becoming a poet in the evenings
to write about lost relations
to mention, obliquely, the undeclared,
the leftovers from failed unions,
the prodigals warranting fatted calves –
we allow ourselves to forget
the hard slog of the ones who stayed at home

come away sunshine

come away Sunshine, pulling on his shirt tail, they'll go ya! two small boys sidle into a shadowed gully before they are seen –

the scrappy group of youths jostle, cigarette packets sitting with tattoos in rolled shirt sleeves on hopeful biceps, elbowing each other, fists up, mock fighting, chiacking, sledging and slamming, passing on their way to the used car yard

he's a pirate
at home drinking chai
flag still flying
but becalmed on the rocks
he's not talking to his sons

Goths

it was in the times the Goths rose at dusk
to eat handfuls of dry breakfast cereal and roam the streets
of Civic with white faces and lips outlined in black
hair in hanks dyed to the required darkness
eyes deep-set with worldly fatigue and mascara –
look for Gothdating.com   to connect with Goths near you
reach out to the Goth community
Contact Us stretched to breaking point with the demands
of Goth singles

the mirror

she creates her public face
in eleven steps
on Goth white foundation
draws Goth tattoos in black

Iced

This summer morning, we know there is ice on the street worth millions.
Ice – meth in the blood makes us crazy – craziness behind the wheel kills us, turning us into national statistics.
The discomfort of infinity, uneasiness with eternity, is obliterated with the urgency of now, wanting it now…
We are beautifully turned out, sartorial turning out, in turning out, coming out with cash wadded into fashionably torn jeans,
waiting for the word on the street…the word is eternity, the length of dying and being dead.

word is
ice on the street
causes road deaths
we once used shovels
now we avoid some corners

Ice

I robbed in the street to buy ice she said
I picked up a felony she said
It was bad.
But then I found some great people
and ice was everywhere,
as much as I wanted,
for free.

Lengthen the hem

The assistant: bosom, name tag, scarlet nails
waits, making a point of patience, sighs.

The wide counter is crowded with stacked
multi-patterned bolts of cloth, tethered scissors
displays of coloured thread and cotton reels
counter edge fixed with a measuring tape in inches.

The woman stands back, stolid, a sudden shaft of sunlight
shows up her worn black coat,
dust motes desultory around a dark headscarf.
She takes from her bag a bundle of fabric,
smoothes it on the edge of the counter –
my daughter-in-law's dress she says
I need something to sew around the hem
to lengthen it.

How can a few unresolved chin hairs

How can a few unresolved chin hairs mean,
as my mother believes,
that I have let myself go?
Or is it liberation that sprouts freely
with menopause?

doll found in trunk

dress up to the nines
all dolled up, cry on demand
put on your glad rags –
you are his living doll –
his to lock up in a trunk

Source: song, Cliff Richard and the Young Ones, 'Living Doll', 1963

I quail before your peacock gaze

No one warned me
how beautiful you had become.
I quail before your peacock gaze
your swagger and swank
and magnificent plumage.

I shy and shrink under the
look-only-at-me sternness of your eye,
cringe and cower, just a common quail
whose camouflage failed,
in the moment, to shield me.

No one warned me of your beauty.

Dark net

if I feel someone is watching me
I go to the web where I am not in this world
the dark place, space, net
that keeps you in the dark
get past my encryption to find me
there you know I can be seen but not found

touch question

who sleeps at night?
we cannot mend the earth with coal and concrete
or Trojan horse of nuclear power plants

how did we know the wind brings storm and dust?
when did we know the ocean cannot clean itself?
why do we say again and again
we did nothing wrong?

I touch, lightly brushing my fingertips,
words on pages that are not in books
roll the grit of them between thumb and forefinger

request a wake-up call when I know I am awake
read my touch scream…

Mainline west

out there
on the mainline west
they stopped listening
'they' turned 'we' to 'you'
and did not notice
when the internet
disappeared

out there
past the nature strip
they stopped conversation
'they' turned 'we' to 'you'
and did not notice
when democracy
disappeared

out there
inside our own heads
the world was afraid
'they' turned 'we' to 'you'
and did not notice
when sanity
disappeared

dangerous to our country

Edward Snowden in the United States leaked classified information from the National Security Agency to mainstream media from June 2013. In a video link from Russia where he was given asylum he explained why. It is now obvious that the move by Western governments to enact data surveillance and retention laws relating to ordinary citizens is contrary to the rule of law and to other hard-won freedoms in the democratic polity…

She is still in the orange paper jumpsuit and too-tight handcuffs. Sounds of Johnny Cash intermittent from the reception counter when someone brings coffee for the desk officers. In the cell darkness, no windows, cold air. In the best of worlds, she is creating a fashion statement. In this world she is out of power, and out of freedoms. She is in orange. It's not the new black.

placards protest
data collection
retention laws
can we all be
dangerous to our country?

at Maralinga

the mushroom cloud burst
thrust to the future
tribes looked up   breathed in dust
scientists turned their backs

in a country that is yours
a place we claim as ours
a place we think we should prevail
…we colonised
Gallipoli is the new Bali

Boots on the ground

all-world all-nation problems
number crunching for profit margins
to generations of youth taken by the military
from bums on seats
to boots on the ground,
the body count goes on
we should ask who –
whose feet in whose boots?
whose bottoms in shiny pants
generations rubbing smooth the splintered wood?
this is what we ask in Sydney
I think it's the same in Syria

In the Hindu Kush

breathe in
breathe out
old light
light years of travel
to reach us
unfolding remembering
old light
comes from beginnings
as well as endings
breathe in
breathe out

the black SUV follows us into the sky, as we climb into the peaks of the Hindu Kush, through the Salang tunnel down into northern Afghanistan.

in the Hindu Kush,
heading for Shiberghan, past Mazar-e-sharif
      our eyes meet in the mirror, both looking back,
Fawad frowning…we look back again
black cars, black windows,
right on our bumper for the last thirty minutes
we are in Dostum's country –
three-car convoy pulls out, passes us, horn blaring,
driver's hand flicking at us through the side window…
a warlord…
      we're in his way, and he's late.

children dance

on a rusted Russian tank
in a rain shower
metal glints in long grass…
landmines forgotten

can democracy

happen on the streets   thumbprints
smudging vote papers?
UN Council's five members
our world's biggest arms suppliers

The soldiers and the tea boy

The evils in the world
come to light in subtle and unexpected ways.
A soldier in the shadows sits close beside the wall.

The foreign soldiers, clumsy on the carpets,
reluctantly, pushing forward their strategy,
pursuing hearts and minds.

The warlord offers them his tea-boy.
As required by tradition and hospitality,
but reluctantly, he pushes the boy forward –
delicate, beautiful, kohl-rimmed eyes,
small hands shaking, fingers tight around the bowl of sweets.

They all stop, jolted, in shock…

Suddenly, all are standing,
tension and outrage around the circle.

All masculinities in the room are outraged.
Honour affronted on all sides,
fury in the impugning of every masculinity.
Fragile tea glasses are crushed into the carpet by heavy boots.
The circle, slowly stepping backwards,
watchful withdrawal on all sides,
all observed by the soldier in the shadows.

Later, in the barracks, relaxing,
tension draining into the shadows,
three die and one runs, jumping the wall.
Another green on blue.

Now, today, yesterday.

Years from now, then, although I should not,
will I say I have forgotten
the green on blue,
the betrayal of trust?
After, away from the dust,
the blood on stone,
because I must,
will I say I am glad
it was you not me,
and I have forgotten,
years from yesterday?

Migration

in a place
where one cow is a farm
and, if it rains, bomb craters
collect water for grazing village goats,
the people are gone

in a place
on the other side of a wall
of razor wire, border guards
shift weapons from hand to hand
watching the oncoming crowd

in a place
where cars and coffee are consumed
without thought, travel-grimed walkers
with empty stomachs are driven to the next border
by concerned citizens

in a place
where a trickle becomes a torrent
as flood gates are opened
laws are made in haste
to prosecute those who take them in

stations of the northern road (1)

Reflected in the water draining on the roadside, they walk for hours around the new border fences, from Syria. The train stations and border posts become familiar names in new languages

Istanbul
Lesbos
Athens
Idomeni
Budapest
Salzburg
Nickelsdorf
Berlin
Paris
Calais

and the town squares and border checkpoints become the words of the language of asylum.

At every roadside relief stop, at every running water tap, in every wayside shelter, the pieces of brown paper, raggy strips of corrugated cardboard torn off the sides of cartons, are pinned, tied, nailed to makeshift message boards. The faces of the signs depend on the weather. They hang sodden, dripping, tearing at the corners; they crisp and curl, peeling back from themselves in the burning sun.

They chronicle in pencil and marker pen the search of Palwasha for her two children separated at the beach when a boat overturned. They tell Adnan to find Amira at the town square station in Budapest, and that Tarek passed through on his way to Nickelsdorf with Salwar's child and Rafi's wife and sister.

Among the tens of thousands of people on the roads, can we
find one particular person or glimpse one particular known face?

The news media photo gallery shows the moving migration,
one by one and group by group, photos composed for effect,
composed to document, to move us –

in pouring rain
coloured plastic ponchos
they cross a border

against the wall
on flattened cardboard cartons
they sit in a square in Athens

at another border
in the mud, all humanity on the move –
a boy in a blue shirt

cordons of riot police
clothes drying on lines in fog
queues stretch back out of sight

show papers
lie down on plastic sheets
it's all temporary –

play when you can
girl in pink on the railway track
walk when you have to

hidden by graffiti
sitting under plastic against the wall –
rainstorm on the trek north

stations of the northern road (2)

found person brown

It starts with terrorism. No, it starts with the arrogance of power. No, no, it starts with genocide. No, and no again. It starts with colonial arrogance. No, it starts with religion and imperialism and western decadence and eastern intransigence… And ethnocentric privileging of who *we* are and *you* are not.

…and the murder of more civilians than you can count, just to emphasise the point.

What point!

The point is, it's all linked. It's all the same evil. The killing of the populations. The running away to a transient mirage of safety. The turning our backs. The millions on the move away from evil, towards rejection and indifference.

Again the question: among the tens of thousands on the roads can we find one particular person or glimpse one particular known face?

I went to the boundary fence
thousands on the migration road
saw a sign
found
        person
                brown

I went to a beach
where clothes and shoes and bags
lie half hidden under sand
tides
  capsize
    boats

I went to buy a record
when I was not yet grown
heard a song
it takes
  more than guns
    to kill a man

I went to a Kalashnikov concert
about Syria in Paris
saw another execution
spread sand
  to soak up
    blood

I went to the Place de la République
for evidence of revolution
saw people eating dinner killed
found
  person
    brown

From the sixties real Australians say welcome to refugees

Real Australians say welcome. I come from the sixties and I know where you come from. Our country of suburban blandness with remnants of Italy and Greece, and Vietnam, hiding self-serving racism barely skin deep, is seasoned now with Africa and the Middle East.

I come from the sixties and what we did for revolution, it all seems so small now. But, sometimes you have to carry something a long way to hold it up and see it properly. From the sixties we know we must sing the fight, and not wait for the powerful to forgive us. We say welcome to asylum seekers. We say welcome to refugees.

if you wonder
about Australia's policies
on rejecting asylum
Dylan and Baez can reach you
from the radio

Just part of the tragedy

Just part of the tragedy is that before they get on the boats,
in their hundreds they stand on the beach holding up their
phones to the stars like a salute, looking for a satellite,
needing bars for a signal and hoping for enough battery to
make a call…
Do they ring their past to say goodbye or ring their future to
alert their coming?
Part of the tragedy is the journey between – for those on
the beach, a ride that may, at any moment, take their breath
away.
Just part of the tragedy is that ringing for help as the boat fills
with water in sight of the landing point will bring the officials
to force the boat to turn around…
So twenty boats in secrecy, mobile phones out of battery
and signal bars unlit are pushed back across a line drawn in
water…

flat bread splashed
with salt water turns to dough
she chews and swallows
one hand braced on the gunnel
against the swell of ocean

laughing

for Bassam Youssef, Egypt, fled to Dubai 2015

I learned the revolution through satire
we questioned everything
the authorities came to hate us
we saw them closing in

we laughed at them with ridicule
we made our revolution by laughing
and making others laugh
laughing taught us everything

I worry now about every child on the road
children question everything
they learn the revolution by laughing –

every child on the road knows the authorities are closing in

transition

ten days talking
still, endorsement by the nations
is tentative –
what will it take for us all
to agree to save ourselves?
we stand in crisped grass
spatter of rain pocks the dust
wind burns skin
looking up for the Rain God –
send 'er down Hughie!

two degrees

or ten degrees rising
Brisbane and Sydney
will slip under the waves
unless a treaty binds us

El Niño

and La Niña
struggle
in the grey area of standing water
mining and artesian basin

Crops

climate change
cramps the style
of crop growth
even if it rains again
will the seeds show green?

heavy machines
parked in a line on dry dirt
no rain
will there be crops again
for us to fire the engines?

he's out cropping
she's home crimping her hair
it's the weekend
they take the ute to town
spend money they don't have

photograph
farmer's family in black and white
on the margin
a shoulder in a dark suit
do we know who was cropped out?

Eyes closed

it was the last time and it had already happened –
events moved so quickly her eyes could not focus

the mandarins hung, orange on thick leaved branches
ripened overnight and fell into cold morning grass

bulldozers and bobcats rev, engines screaming
metal on live, growing, green wood

she screws her eyes shut against the noise
stink of rising dust –

before she had made the tea the orchard was gone

About the Author

In 2015 Sandra Renew published poems in:
- *One Last Border: Poems for refugees*, Hazel Hall, Moya Pacey and Sandra Renew, Ginninderra Press
- *Flood, Fire and Drought*, edited by Suzanne Edgar, Kathleen Kituai, Sandra Renew and Hazel Hall, Ginninderra Press, 2015; showcasing the work of twenty-nine Australian poets, and with a foreword by Dr Richard Denniss, this anthology explores the effect of weather events on the Australian landscape
- *Projected on the Wall*, poems by Sandra Renew, Ginninderra Press, Pocket Poets series
- *This is why*, a chapbook of poems of protest by Sandra Renew

www.ingramcontent.com/pod-product-compliance
Lightning Source LLC
Chambersburg PA
CBHW062204100526
44589CB00014B/1947